CATHOLIC CATECHISM

First Holy Communion

Revised edition

TABLE OF CONTENT

iv

CHAPTER ONE

PRAYERS

(No special time should be set aside for teaching formal prayers. The following prayers should be taught in the Bible context or in Lesson form. Our kids should be guided and encouraged to pray in their own words regularly)

THE SIGN OF THE CROSS

(We sanctify and consecrate our lives to the three persons

of the Blessed Trinity; CCC232-234)

In the name of the Father, and of the Son and of the Holy

Spirit.   Amen.

OUR LORD'S PRAYER

Matthew 6:5-15	Mark 11:24-26	Luke 11: 1-13

Jesus Teaches Us To Pray   *CCC 2777-2853*

Our Father, who art in heaven, hallow be thy name; thy kingdom come; thy will be done on earth as it is in heaven. Give us our daily bread; and forgive us our trespasses as we forgive those who trespass against us; and lead us not into temptation, but deliver us from evil. Amen

Luke 1:26-56	*The birth of Jesus announced; Mary visits Elizabeth*

CCC 2673-2679

Hail Mary, full of grace,

the Lord is with thee.

Blessed art thou amongst women,

and blessed is the fruit of thy womb, Jesus.

Holy Mary, Mother of God,

pray for us sinners,

now and at the hour of our death. Amen

GLORY BE TO THE FATHER

GLORY BE TO THE FATHER

Luke 2: 8-20	The Shepherds and the angels

Glory be to the Father, and to the Son: and to the Holy

Ghost;

As it was in the beginning, is now, and ever shall be:

world without end. Amen.

THE NICENE CREED

I believe in one God, the Father Almighty,

Maker *of heaven and earth, and* of all things visible and

invisible.

I believe in one Lord Jesus Christ, the *only-begotten* Son

of God, born of the Father before all ages. God from God,

Light of Light, very God of very God, begotten, not made,

consubstantial with the Father

by whom all things were made

who for us men, and for our salvation, came down *from*

heaven, and was incarnate *by the Holy Ghost and of the*

Virgin Mary, and was made man he *was crucified for us*

under Pontius Pilate, and suffered, *and was buried,* and

the third day he rose again, *according to the Scriptures,*

and ascended into heaven, *and sit on the right hand of*

the Father; from thence he shall come *again, with glory,*

to judge the quick and the dead. *;whose kingdom shall*

have no end.

And in the Holy Ghost, *the Lord and Giver of life, who proceed from the Father, who with the Father and the Son together is worshiped and glorified, who spake by the prophets*

In *one* holy catholic and apostolic Church; we acknowledge one baptism for the remission of sins; we look for the resurrection of the dead, and the life of the world to come. Amen.

THE APOSTLES' CREED

I believe in God, the Father almighty, creator of heaven and earth. I believe in Jesus Christ, his only Son, our Lord. He was conceived by the power of the Holy Spirit and born of the virgin Mary. He suffered under Pontius Pilate, was crucified, died, and was buried. He descended to the dead. On the third day he rose again. He ascended into heaven, and is seated at the right hand of the Father. He will come again to judge the living and the dead. I believe in the Holy Spirit, the holy catholic Church, the communion of the saints, the forgiveness of sins, the resurrection of the body, and the life everlasting. Amen

I confess to almighty god and to you my brothers and sisters that I have greatly sinned in my thoughts and in my thoughts and in my words, in what I have done and in what I have failed to do, through my faults, through my faults, through my most grievous fault; therefore I ask Blessed Mary ever-virgin, all the Angels and Saints and you my brothers and sisters to pray for me to the Lord our God.

THE GLORIA

It may be said or Sung

Glory to God in the highest, and on earth peace to people of good will. We praise you, we bless you, we adore you, we glorify you, we give you thanks for your great glory, Lord God, heavenly King, O God almighty Father. Lord Jesus Christ, Only Begotten Son, Lord God, Lamb of God, Son of the Father, you take away the sins of the world, have mercy on us; you take away the sins of the world, receive our prayer; you are seated at the right hand of the Father, have mercy on us. For You alone are the Holy One, you alone are the Lord, you alone are the Most High, Jesus Christ, with the Holy Spirit, in the glory of God the Father. Amen

THE ANGEL GUARDIAN

Angel of God, my guardian dear, Whom God's love commits me here, Ever this day (night) be at my side, To light and guard, to rule and guide.

HAIL HOLY QUEEN

John 2: 1-12	The Marriage feast at Cana

Hail, holy Queen, Mother of Mercy,

Hail our life, our sweetness and our hope.

To thee do we cry,

Poor banished children of Eve;

To thee do we send up our sighs,

Mourning and weeping in this valley of tears.

Turn then, most gracious advocate,

Thine eyes of mercy toward us;

And after this our exile,

Show unto us the blessed fruit of thy womb, Jesus.

O clement, O loving,

O sweet Virgin Mary.

SHORT ACTS OF FAITH, HOPE AND CHARITY

1Thess 1:2-4; 3:6-10	1Corinthians 13:13;	Colossians 1:3-8
Ephesians 1:15-	Hebrew 10:23-24	John 4:7-12

21		

ACT OF FAITH

My God, I believe in You and all that Your Church teaches,

because You have said it and your word is true.

ACT OF HOPE

My God, I hope in You, for grace and for glory, because of

Your promises, Your mercy and Your power.

ACT OF CHARITY

My God, because You are so good, I love You with all my

heart, and for Your sake, I love my neighbor as myself.

ACT OF CONTRITION (SHORT FORM)

Luke 18:9-14	Pharisee and the Publican

Luke 15: 11-32	The Prodigal Son

O my God, I am sorry for all my sins, because they displease You, Who are All good and deserving of all my love. With Your help, I will sin no more.

O my God, I am heartily sorry for having offended Thee, and I detest all my sins, because I dread the loss of Heaven and the pains of hell, but most of all because they offend Thee, my God, Who art all good and deserving of all my love. I firmly resolve with the help of Thy grace to confess my sins, to do penance, and to amend my life. Amen.

GRACE BEFORE MEAL

Bless us, O Lord, and these Thy gifts, which we are about to receive from Thy bounty, through Christ our Lord, Amen.

We give You thanks, almighty God for these and all the benefits which we have received from Your bounty through Christ our Lord, Amen.

Luke 1: 26-38	The Annunciation

CCC 490-495

L. **The Angel of the Lord declared unto Mary,**
R. And she conceived of the Holy Spirit.

Hail Mary, etc...

L. **Behold the handmaid of the Lord.**
R. Be it done unto me according to Your Word.

Hail Mary, etc...

L. **And the Word was made flesh,**

R. And dwelt among us.

Hail Mary, etc...

L. **Pray for us, O holy Mother of God.**

R. That we may be made worthy of the promises of Christ.

Let us pray:

Pour forth, we beseech You, O Lord,
Your Grace into our hearts;
that we to whom the incarnation of Christ,
your Son was made known by the message of an Angel,
may by His passion and cross
be brought to the glory of His Resurrection.
Through the same Christ, our Lord, Amen.

Holy Michael, the Archangel, defend us in battle. Be our safeguard against the wickedness and snares of the devil. May God rebuke him, we humbly pray; and do you, O Prince of the heavenly host, by the power of God cast into hell Satan and all the evil spirits who wander through the world seeking the ruin of souls. Amen.

THE MEMORARE OF ST. BERNARD

Remember, O most gracious Virgin Mary, that never was it known that any one who fled to thy protection, implored thy help, and sought thy intercession, was left unaided. Inspired with this confidence, I fly unto thee, O Virgin of virgins, my Mother, to thee I come, before thee I stand sinful and sorrowful.

O Mother of the Word Incarnate! despise not my petitions, but, in thy mercy, hear and answer me. Amen

CHAPTER TWO

THE ESSENTIAL CHRISTIAN DOCTRINES

THE TEN COMMANDMENTS

1. I am the Lord your God; you shall not have strange gods before Me.

2. You shall not take the Name of the Lord your God in vain.

3. Remember to keep holy the Lord's day.

4. Honor your father and your mother.

5. You shall not kill.

6. You shall not commit adultery.

7. You shall not steal.

8. You shall not bear false witness against your neighbour.

9. You shall not covet your neighbour's wife.

10. You shall not covet your neighbour's goods.

THE TWO GREATEST COMMANDMENTS

i.   You shall love the Lord your God with your whole heart, and with your whole soul, and with all your mind.

ii.   You shall love your neighbor as yourself

THE PRECEPTS OF THE CHURCH

I.   To assist at Mass on all Sundays and holy days of obligation.

II.   To fast and abstain on the days appointed.

III.   To confess our sins at least once a year.

IV.   To receive Holy Communion during the Easter time.

V.   To contribute to the support of the Church.

VI.   To observe the laws of the Church concerning marriage

THE SEVEN CORPORAL WORKS OF MERCY

i.   To feed the hungry

ii.   To give water to the thirsty

iii.   To clothe the naked

iv.   To shelter the homeless

v.   To visit the sick

vi.   To visit the imprisoned

vii.   To bury the dead

THE SEVEN SPIRITUAL WORKS OF MERCY

i.   To counsel the doubtful

ii.   To instruct the ignorant

iii.   To admonish the sinner

iv.   To comfort the sorrowful

v.   To forgive all injuries

vi.   To bear wrongs patiently

vii.   To pray for the living and the dead

THE THREE ESSENTIAL GOOD WORKS

i.   Prayer

ii.   Fasting

iii. Almsgiving

THE SEVEN GIFTS OF THE HOLY SPIRIT

I.   Wisdom

II.   Understanding

III. Counsel

IV.   Fortitude

V.   Knowledge

VI.   Piety

VII. Fear of the Lord

CHARISMATIC GIFTS OF THE HOLY SPIRITS

i.   Gift of speaking with wisdom

ii.   Gift of speaking with knowledge

iii. Faith

iv.   Grace of Leading

v.   Gift of miracles

vi.   Gift of prophecy

vii. Gift of discerning spirits

viii. Gift of tongues

ix.   Gift of interpreting speeches

THE TWELVE FRUITS OF THE HOLY SPIRIT

i.   Charity

ii.   Joy

iii.   Peace

iv.   Patience

v.   Benignity

vi.   Goodness

vii.   Longanimity

viii. Mildness

ix.   Faith

x.   Modesty

xi.   Continency

xii.   Chastity

THE THREE THEOLOGICAL VIRTUES

i.   Faith

ii.   Hope

iii.   Charity

THE FOUR CARDINAL VIRTUES

i.   Prudence

ii.   Justice

iii.   Fortitude

iv.   Temperance

THE SEVEN CAPITAL SINS

i.   Pride

ii.   Greed

iii.   Lust

iv.   Anger

v.   Gluttony

vi.   Envy

vii.   Sloth

THE SIX SINS AGAINST THE HOLY SPIRIT

i.   Presumption

ii.   Despair

iii.   Resisting the known truth

iv.   Envy of another's spiritual good

v.   Obstinancy in sin

vi.   Final impenitence.

CONDITIONS FOR MORTAL SIN

i.   Grave matter

ii.   Full knowledge

iii.   Deliberate consent

i.   By counsel

ii.   By command

iii.   By consent

iv.   By provocation

v.   By praise or flattery

vi.   By concealment

vii.   By Partaking

viii.   By silence

ix.   By defense of ill done

THE THREE EVANGELICAL COUNSELS

i.   Voluntary poverty

ii.   Perpetual chastity

iii.   Entire obedience

THE THREE POWERS OF THE SOUL

i.   Memory

ii.   Intellect

iii.   Will

THE FOUR PILLARS OF THE CATHOLIC FAITH

i.   The Apostles Creed

ii.   The Seven Sacraments

iii.   The Ten Commandments

iv.   The Lord's Prayer

THE THREE PILLARS OF THE CHURCH'S AUTHORITY

i.   Sacred Scripture

ii.   Sacred Tradition

iii.   Living Magisterium

THE THREE MUNERA (DUTIES OF THE ORDAINED)

i.   Munus docendi (duty to teach, based on Christ's role as Prophet)

ii.   Munus sanctificandi(duty to sanctify, based on Christ's role as Priest)

iii.   Munus regendi (duty to shephard, based on Christ's role as King).

THE THREE PARTS OF THE CHURCH

i.   The church militants (Christians on Earth)

ii.   The Church Suffering (Christians in Purgatory)

iii.   The Church Triumphant (Christians in Heaven)

THE FOUR MARKS OF THE CHURCH

i.   Unity

ii.   Sanctity

iii.   Catholicity

iv.   Apostolicity

i. Blessed are the poor in spirit; for theirs is the kingdom of Heaven

ii. Blessed are the meek; for they shall posses the land.

iii. Blessed are they who mourn: for they shall be comforted.

iv. Blessed are they that hunger and thirst after justice: for they shall have their fill.

v. Blessed are the merciful: for they shall obtain mercy.

vi. Blessed are the pure in heart; for they shall see God.

vii. Blessed are the peacemakers; for they shall be called children of God.

viii.   Blessed are they that suffer persecution for justice' sake for theirs is the Kingdom of Heaven.

STATIONS OF THE CROSS

1. Jesus is condemned to death
2. Jesus takes up his Cross
3. Jesus falls for the first time
4. Jesus meets his Mother
5. Simon of Cyrene helps Jesus carry the Cross
6. Veronica wipes the face of Jesus
7. Jesus falls for the second time
8. Jesus meets the women of Jerusalem
9. Jesus falls for the third time
10. Jesus is stripped of his garments
11. Jesus is nailed to the Cross
12. Jesus dies on the Cross
13. Jesus is taken down from the Cross
14. Jesus is laid in the tomb

Seraphim

These are the highest order or choir of angels. They are the angels who are attendants or guardians before God's throne. They praise God, calling, "Holy Holy Holy is the Lord of Hosts". the only Bible reference is Isaiah 6:1-7. One of them touched Isaiah's lips with a live coal from the altar, cleansing him from sin. Seraphim have six wings, two cover their faces, two cover their feet, and two are for flying.

Cherubim

Cherubim rank after the seraphim and are the second highest in the nine hierarchies or choirs of angels. The Old Testament does not reveal any evidence that the Jews considered them as intercessors or helpers of God. They were closely linked in God's glory. They are manlike in appearance and double-winged and were guardians of God's glory. They symbolized then, God's power and mobility. In the New Testament, they are alluded to as celestial attendants in the Apocalypse (Rv 4-6). Catholic tradition describes them as angels who have an intimate knowledge of God and continually praise Him.

Thrones

Thrones are the Angels of pure Humility, Peace and Submisssion. They reside in the area of the cosmos where material form begins to take shape. The lower Choir of Angels need the Thrones to access God.

Dominions

Dominions are Angels of Leadership. They regulate the duties of the angels, making known the commands of God.

Virtues

Virtues are known as the Spirits of Motion and control the elements. They are sometimes referred to as "the shining ones." They govern all nature. They have control over seasons, stars, moon; even the sun is subject to their command. They are also in charge of miracles and provide courage, grace, and valor.>

Powers

Powers are Warrior Angels against evil defending the cosmos and humans. They are known as potentates. They fight against evil spirits who attempt to wreak chaos through human beings. The chief is said to be either Samael or Camael, both angels of darkness.

Archangels

Archangels are generally taken to mean "chief or leading angel" (Jude 9; 1 Thes 4:16), they are the most frequently mentioned throughout the Bible. They may be of this or other hierarchies as St. Michael Archangel, who is a princely Seraph. The Archangels have a unique role as God's messenger to the people at critical times in history and salvation (Tb 12:6, 15; Jn 5:4; Rv 12:7-9) as in The Annunciation and Apocalypse. A feast day celebrating the Archangels Michael, Gabriel and Raphael is celebrated throughout the Church Sep 29. A special part of the Byzantine Liturgy invokes the "Cherubic Hymn" which celebrates these archangels and the guardian angels particularly.

Of special significance is St. Michael as he has been invoked as patron and protector by the Church from the time of the Apostles. The Eastern Rite and many others place him over all the angels, as Prince of the Seraphim. He is described as the "chief of princes" and as the leader of the forces of heaven in their triumph over Satan and his followers. The angel Gabriel first appeared in the Old Testament in the prophesies of Daniel, he announced the prophecy of 70 weeks (Dn 9:21-27). He appeared to Zechariah to announce the birth of St. John the Baptist (Lk 1:11). It was also Gabriel which proclaimed the Annunciation of Mary to be the mother of our Lord and Saviour. (Lk 1:26) The angel Raphael first appeared in the book of Tobit (Tobias)Tb 3:25, 5:5-28, 6-12). He announces "I am the Angel Raphael, one of the seven who stand before the throne of God." (Tb 12:15)

Principalities

In the New Testament Principalities refers to one type of spiritual (metaphysical) being which are now quite hostile to God and human beings. (Rom 8:38; 1 Cor 15:24; Eph 1:21; 3:10; 6:12; Col 1:16; 2:10, 15) Along with the principalities are the powers (Rom 8:38; 1 Cor 15:24; Eph 1:21; 1 Pt 3:22; 2 Thes 1:7); and cosmological powers (1 Cor 15:24; Eph 1:21; 3:10; Col 2:15);Dominions (Eph 1:21; Col 1:16) and thrones (Col1:16). The clarity of the New

Testament witness helps see that these beings were created through Christ and for Him (Col 1:16). Given their hostility to God and humans due to sin, Christ's ultimate rule over them (ibid) expresses the reign of the Lord over all in the cosmos. This is the Lordship of Christ, which reveals God's tremendous salvation in conquering sin and death at the cross, and now takes place in the Church. (Eph 3:10)

Angels

These angels are closest to the material world and human begins. They deliver the prayers to God and God's answers and other messages to humans. Angels have the capacity to access any and all other Angels at any time. They are the most caring and social to assist those who ask for help.

THE SEVEN LAST WORDS OF CHRIST

i.　　Father, forgive them for they know not what they do (Luke 23:34)

ii.   Amen I say to thee: This day thou shalt be with me in paradise (Luke 23:43)

iii.   Woman, behold thy son. Son behold thy mother (John 19:26-27)

iv.   Eli, Eli Lamma sabacthani? (My God, My God, why hast Thou forsaken me?) (Matthew 27:46, ref Psalm 21)

v.   I thirst (John 19:28)

vi.   It is finished (John 19:30)

vii.   Father, into Thy hands I commend my spirit (Luke 23:46, ref Psalm 30:6)

CHAPTER THREE

GOD OUR FATHER

GOD MADE EVERYTHING

Genesis 1-2	Creation story

CCC 279-373

I. Who made all things?

II.   God made all things

III. Why did God make all things?

IV.   God made all things because God loves us.

V. What great gift did God give to Adam and Eve?

VI.   God gave Adam and Eve the great gift of His own life.

VII. Who made you?

VIII.   God made me.

IX. Why did God make you?

God made me to know Him, to love Him, and to serve Him in this world and to be happy with Him forever in Heaven.

Genesis 2:15-17	God commanded man not to eat the fruit of the tree of knowledge

CCC 387, 1440

I. What is sin?

II. **Sin is turning away from God's love.**

III. How did God punish Adam and Eve for their sins?

IV. **God punish Adam and Eve for their sins by taking away the gift of His life.**

V. Why did God promise Adam and Eve a savior?

VI. **God promised Adam and Eve a savior because he still loved them.**

CHAPTER FOUR

OUR LORD JESUS CHRIST

THE PROMISE OF A REDEEMER

Genesis 3:1-14	The disobedience of man

CCC 389

I. How did God show His great love and mercy after Adam's sin?

II. **God showed His great love and mercy by His promise to send a Savior.**

III. What was the promised Savior to do?

IV. **The promised savior was to win back for all humans the gift of God's Life which has been lost by Sin.**

OUR SAVIOR IS BORN

Luke 1:26-36	The birth of the Savior announced
Luke 2:1-20	The birth of Christ

CCC 484-486

I. Who is Jesus Christ?

II. **Jesus Christ is the Son of God, the Second Person of the Blessed Trinity, true God and true man.**

III. How many Persons are there in God?

IV. **There are three Persons In God- the Father, the Son and the Holy Spirit.**

V. What is te name of the Son of God made man?

VI. **The name of the Son of God made man is Jesus Christ.**

VII. Who is the Mother of Jesus Christ?

VIII. **The Mother of Jesus Christ is the Blessed Virgin Mary.**

IX. When do we celebrate the birth of Jesus Christ?

X. **We celebrate the birth of Jesus Christ on Christmas Day.**

JESUS PLEASED GOD IN EVERYTHING.

Luke 2:51	Jesus went down with them
John 14:31	I do as the Father has commanded me
John 13:15	I have given you an example

CCC 599-618

I. How did Jesus Christ save the world?

II.   **Jesus Christ saved the world by offering His Life on the Cross.**

III.   Why did Jesus Christ suffer and die?

IV.   **Jesus Christ suffered and died for our sins.**

V.   On what day did Jesus die?

VI.   **Jesus died on Good Friday.**

VII.   What happened to Jesus after His death?

VIII.   **After His death, God the Father raised Jesus from the dead.**

IX.   On what day do we celebrate the resurrection of Jesus?

X.   **We celebrate the resurrection of Jesus on Easter Sunday.**

CHAPTER FIVE

1. WHAT IS SACRAMENT?

   A sacrament is:

   i. **A visible sign**

   ii. **Signifying the gift of God's grace**

   iii. **Given by Jesus Christ.**

2. Which are the seven sacraments?

   The seven sacraments are:

   i. **Baptism**

   ii. **Confirmation**

   iii. **Holy Eucharist**

   iv. **Penance**

   v. **Anointing of the sick**

   vi. **Holy Orders**

   vii. **Holy Matrimony**

CHAPTER SIX

THE SACRAMENT OF BAPTISM

2Kings 5:1-15	Naaman the Syrian is cleansed	Titus 3:5
John 3:5	Matthew 28:19-20	Mark 16:15-16

CCC 1213-1274

1. What is Baptism?

    Baptism is the sacrament which takes away original sin, and gives us a new life, the life of God, making us children of God.

2. When does Jesus make us children of God?

    Jesus makes us children of God when we are baptized.

3. What must I do to keep God's life?

    To keep God's life I must live as a true child of God.

4. How can I live as a true child of God?

I can live as a true child of God always living

a life pleasing to God.

CHAPTER SEVEN

THE SACRAMENT OF HOLY EUCHARIST

1. What is the sacrament of Holy Eucharist?

    The sacrament of Holy Eucharist is Jesus GIFT of Himself to us at the Last Supper, on the night before He died. He gave Himself with the words: "This is my Body; This is my Blood"

    Matthew 26:26-28

2. What is Holy Communion?

    Eating the Body and drinking the Blood of Jesus under the form of bread and wine is called Holy Communion.

CHAPTER EIGHT

THE SACRAMENT OF PENANCE AND RECONCILLIATION

1. SIN OFFENDS GOD OUR LOVING FATHER

Luke 15:11-24	The Prodigal Son

CCC 1422-1470

i. When do we sin?

We sin when we do something wrong on purpose.

ii. Why does sin offend God?

Sin offends God because when we sin we do not love God.

iii. How many kinds of sins are there?

There are two kinds of sins: Original sin and Personal sins

iv. What is Original Sin?

Original sin is the sin of disobedience to God committed by our first parents,

Adam and Eve. Since all of us inherit this sinful nature of our first parents all are born in this state of broken relationship with God.

v.   What are Personal Sins?

Personal sins are the sins we commit knowingly. These can be mortal or venial.

vi.   What is a mortal sin?

A mortal sin is offending God knowingly and willingly in a serious matter.

vii.   What is a venial sin?

A venial sin is offending God in a small matter, knowingly and willingly.

viii.   What does mortal sin do to the soul?

Mortal sin takes away God's life from the soul until the person asks God for forgiveness.

ix.   What does venial sin do to the soul?

**Venial sins do not take away God's life,
but they make our love for God weaker.**

2. JESUS, HELP ME

Matthew 4:1-11	The Temptation of our Lord in the desert.
Matthew 26:41	Watch and pray

i.   What is temptation?

**Temptation is an enticement to commit
sin or to do something wrong.**

ii.   What must I do when I am tempted?

**When I am tempted I must ask Jesus to
help me to do what is right even when it
is hard for me.**

iii.   Who helps us to fight temptations?

Jesus helps us to fight temptations.

3. **JESUS GIVES THE APOSTLES THE POWER TO FORGIVE SIN**

John 20:19-23	The risen Jesus gives the apostles power to forgive sins.

i.   To whom has Jesus given the power to forgive sins?

Through the Apostles Jesus has given the priest the power to forgive sins in Confession.

ii.   What must I do to make a good Confession?

To make a good Confession I must:

    i.   Ask God for help to become aware of my sins. (See Appendix 1 on Examination of Conscience.)

    ii.   Ask God for the grace to be really sorry for my sins.

    iii.   Promise God to do better.

iv.   **Tell all my sis to the priest.**

v.   **Do the penance the priest gives me.**

vi.   **Thank God for forgiving me my sins.**

iii.   What is the most important part of Confession?

The most important part of Confession is to be sincerely sorry for my sins; for, without sorrow my sins cannot be forgiven.

iv.   How do you make your Confession?

I make my Confession in this way:

i.   **I kneel, make the sign of the cross and say: Bless me, father, for I have sinned. My last Confession was …. Ago."**

ii.   **I then tell my sins to the priest.**

iii.   I listen to the priest as he forgives me and reply "Amen".

iv.   I do the penance the priest gives me.

v.   I thank God for forgiving me my sins.

APPENDIX I

EXAMINATION OF CONSCIENCE

(for children)

(The following points are a few hints to help the child to be aware of the sins he/she may have committed)

- Did I keep anger and bitterness in my heart?
- Did I grumble when I was corrected or punished?
- Did I refuse to help other children even those who are not in my family or among my friends- especially the poor and the sick?
- Did I try to bluff or tell lies? In this did I hurt anyone?
- Did I spoil another's good name by carrying tales?

- Did I sau my prayers only with my lips without thinking or trying to join myself to God?

- How do I behave in church?

- Do I remember that the church is the place where especially I meet Jesus?

- Am iattentive at Mass and participate in it properly and meaningfully by offering myself together with the bread and wine?

- Have I obeyed my parents?

- Do I remember that my parents and my elders stand in the place of God?

- Do I respect them and listen to them?

- Have I made fun of old or handicapped people?

- Do I take things that do not belong to me?

  (If I have taken anything I should return it before I go to Confession)

- Di I misuse my tongue and my mouth for saying bad words?

- Am I greedy?

- Have I been jealous of others?

APPENDIX II

THANKSGIVING AFTER COMMUNION

Act of Faith: O Jesus, I believe that I have received your Flesh to eat and your Blood to drink, because you have said it, and your word is true.

Act of Adoration: O Jesus, my God, my Creator, I adore you, because from your hands I came and with you I am to be happy for ever.

Act of Love: Sweet Jesus, I love you; I love you with all my heart. You know that I love you, and wish to love you daily more and more.

Act of Thanksgiving: My good Jesus, I thank you with all my heart. How good, how kind you are to me, sweet Jesus! Blessed be Jesus in the most holy Sacrament of the Altar.

Act of Offering: O Jesus, receive my poor offering.

Jesus, you have given yourself to me, and now let

me give myself to you.

I give you my body, that it may be chaste ad pure.

I give you my soul, that it may be free from sin.

I give you my heart, that it may always love you.

I give you every breath that I shall breathe, and

especially my last; I give myself in life and in death,

that I may be yours for ever and ever.

SOUL OF CHRIST

Soul of Christ, sanctify me.

Body of Christ, save me.

Blood of Christ, inebriate me.

Water from the side of Christ, wash me.

Passion of Christ, strengthen me.

O good Jesus, hear me.

Within your wounds hide me.

Never let me be separated from you.

From the wicked enemy defend me.

In the hour of my death, call me.

And bid me come to you,

So that with your saints

I may praise you forever and ever,

Amen.